LET'S HAVE LUNCH

Double Lunching

LET'S HAVE LUNCH

GAMES OF SEX AND POWER

by Louise Bernikow

Illustrations by Marc Rosenthal
Designed by Milton Glaser

HARMONY BOOKS/NEW YORK

Copyright © 1981 by Louise Bernikow
Illustrations copyright © 1981 by Marc Rosenthal

Inquiries should be addressed to Harmony Books, a division of Crown Publishers, Inc., One Park Avenue, New York, New York 10016. Harmony Books is a registered trademark of Crown Publishers, Inc.

Jacket and book design by Milton Glaser

Printed in the United States of America

Published simultaneously in Canada by General Publishing Company Limited

Library of Congress Cataloging in Publication Data

Bernikow, Louise, 1940–
  Let's have lunch.

    1. Luncheons.   2. Entertaining.   I. Title.
TX735.B47 1981   394.1   81-6606
ISBN: 0-517-542749   AACR2

10 9 8 7 6 5 4 3 2 1
First Edition

CONTENTS

The Laws

Parkinson's Lunch:

LUNCH EXPANDS TO FILL THE TIME AND
IMPORTANCE ATTACHED TO IT

Peter's Lunch:

ONE LUNCHES UP TO THE LEVEL OF HIS INCOMPETENCE

Billie Holiday's Lunch:

GOD BLESS THE CHILD THAT'S GOT HIS OWN

Murphy's Lunch:

EVERYTHING THAT CAN GO WRONG AT LUNCH DOES

Acton's Lunch:

ABSOLUTE LUNCH CORRUPTS ABSOLUTELY

Gertrude Stein's Lunch:

A LUNCH IS A LUNCH IS A LUNCH

of Lunch 🍎

Hamlet's Lunch:

TO EAT, OR NOT TO EAT: THAT IS THE QUESTION

Newton's Lunch:

EVERY LUNCH HAS AN EQUAL AND OPPOSITE LUNCH

Gresham's Lunch:

BAD LUNCH TENDS TO DRIVE OUT THE GOOD

Anonymous Lunch:

THERE IS NO SUCH THING AS A FREE LUNCH

Heisenberg's Uncertainty Lunch:

ANY OBSERVATION OF LUNCH CHANGES THE LUNCH ITSELF

Tennyson's Lunch:

IT IS BETTER TO HAVE LUNCHED AND LOST
THAN NEVER TO HAVE LUNCHED AT ALL

*W*e are not born lunching.

School teaches us that lunch is a negotiation with the world. Our lunches look better or worse than other kids' lunches. We learn to negotiate: "My papaya for your chocolate chip cookie." We adjust: "I can't bring cornflakes for lunch because the kids will laugh. Besides, it's messy to eat."

Lunch suddenly mirrors the opinions of our peers and measures our self-esteem. It represents the world of making choices and living with the consequences. By adolescence, we have learned to worry about sitting at the right table in the lunchroom. We have become loners, groupies or stars. We have lunch with other people and behave like great kidders or sullen creeps, talkers or listeners, followers or leaders. We have observed the relationship between lunch and style.

Working brings more lessons. The new person on the job is always a lonely luncher. Some cope by hiding in closets munching egg salad sandwiches. Others take to cafeterias, barricaded behind stacks of magazines. Ambitious people learn the rules of the game.

The first thing ambitious people learn is that lunch is political: those who can afford to take the world to lunch eat free, while bus-riding, penny-watching workers have to make their own way. The system can be cracked. The determined ones learn how to weasel in on other people's lunch lives. They acquire credit cards. They get results: clients, contracts, lovers, more lunch invitations. Lunch becomes what they do.

Lunch quickly separates itself from the other meals of the day. It is difficult to swashbuckle at breakfast, where the company is familiar and intolerant of things like lectures in Greek, flashing pinky rings and the promise of deals. Breakfast companions have heard us howl over the toothpaste. These same people have the mundane habit of reappearing at dinner, complaining about math tests, mothers-in-law and cracks in the ceiling. Lunch offers variety and blissful freedom from familiarity.

Lunch expands. It becomes a shot in the arm or a shot in the dark. It elicits the excitement of a blind date or calls for the solemnity of High Mass. Lunch is not a meal but a game. Played with expertise and gusto, it becomes not only the high point of a business day, but, sometimes, even better than life itself.

Chapter One

❧ THE INVITATION ❧

"LET'S HAVE LUNCH": A GRAMMAR

*L*et's have lunch" is a handy phrase. Applied judiciously, it covers any situation, meets any emergency, initiates any activity. It is an appropriate response to any of the following remarks:

"My wife's leaving me."

"I have something interesting on my desk."

"I don't know. We're not getting the kind of results we thought we would get."

🍎 THE LAW OF HIDDEN INTENTIONS: PEOPLE SAY "LET'S HAVE LUNCH" WHEN THEY CAN'T THINK OF ANYTHING ELSE TO SAY OR WHEN THEY MEAN TO SAY SOMETHING ELSE.

The precise form in which someone says "Let's have lunch" reveals whether the phrase is being used as an invitation, an evasion, a stall, a panacea, the first step in a seduction or the killing blow to a love affair.

"I'm pregnant."

"Hey, I'm in the number-two spot now."

"I'll be in town for a week."

"Our building's going co-op."

"If you don't get your troops out of there, we'll blow the place up."

"Let's have lunch" is as useful and malleable as putty. It can unstick a sticky situation, smooth out trouble spots or wedge open an otherwise closed door. Business would grind to a halt without it. Romance would be out of business. Those for whom "Let's have lunch" is a reflex or an afterthought would be struck dumb. There is no better exit line.

"Let's Have Lunch Sometime."

This is evasive. People say it at business parties when they don't know what to say, don't want to look at the new fall line, have not read the script, have no intention of hiring you and wish you wouldn't ask.

People who see each other year after year at the annual convention or sales conferences meet accidentally, feign pleasure, shake hands and close the encounter, saying, "Let's have lunch sometime." Usually, one lives in Oregon and the other in Miami.

Among men and women with no ostensible business between them, this is an insecure invitation. "Lunch" is safer than "dinner." "Sometime" is safer than "Tuesday." A passive form, it leaves the ball and the lunch in the opposite court. Men say this more often than women do.

"We Ought to Have Lunch."

This implies a moral imperative. It is a guilt-inducing invitation. The person who says it is manipulative. The *ought* preys on the mind of the person being addressed. Something must be owed. A favor, perhaps, returned. It is unclear on which side the debt lies, but obligation is surely implied. So is the idea that lunch between the two parties would somehow be for the greater good. Saying "We ought to have lunch" at a time of national crisis, implies that the fate of the nation hangs in the balance. Said by one sex to another, it carries more than a hint of unavoidable romantic destiny.

"How About Lunch?"

Some ways of inviting people to lunch simply beg for wise-guy responses. Asking "How about lunch?" is like asking what someone thinks of the universe. It requires a range of value judgments that most people feel incapable of making. For that reason, the response is usually, "Well, how about it?" The only occasion on which this form makes sense is when both people are scanning their calendars, trying to find a mutually convenient time to meet and each has a "flooded" calendar. "How about lunch?" then becomes a life raft.

"Are You Free for Lunch?"

A straight-man invitation that concentrates unduly on liberty, another concept that makes people uneasy enough to answer with wisecracks. "No, it'll cost ya" is the response that comes too easily to mind. "Nothing's free" or "There is no such thing as a free lunch"—which will be disputed later—are common responses. It creates a severe anxious flutter when said by one sex or another, particularly by men to women. The person who puts the question this way is left confused about whether the invitation has been accepted or refused.

THE PASSING REMARK

*W*hatever linguistic form it takes, the lunch invitation is usually offered as a passing remark in situations that have nothing to do with lunch: as you are climbing into a taxi, talking with the vice-president's wife at a cocktail party, tying your running shoes in the elevator or chewing on a pencil at your desk. The problem is how to take it.

A person being invited to lunch has to decipher the invitation, decide what it really means and whether or not it is serious, then consider whether the answer will be yes, no or maybe.

RESPONDING TO INVITATIONS: PASS INTERCEPTION

*P*romiscuity breeds mistrust. Since "Let's have lunch" is so easily bantered about, the first thing to do upon hearing it is to determine the speaker's sincerity. Gertrude Stein was sincere when she invited people to lunch—a fact easily established by observing that her invitations were almost always followed by actual lunches. Custer shouting "Let's have lunch" to Sitting Bull, or MacArthur muttering it to Tojo probably had a different meaning.

Inability to spot an insincere lunch invitation has left many a poor soul lingering near the telephone. Waiting for a lunch that never materializes is potentially embarrassing. If you tell others that you have been invited to lunch by a known philanderer of the phrase, you will be met with a knowing smirk. Some people are known for saying "Let's have lunch" as frequently as others say "Nuke 'em" or "Never on the first date."

Most people don't know whether or not they want to have lunch with the person who asked them. Some people hold out for dinner. Others want to find out who else will be there or wait to see if something

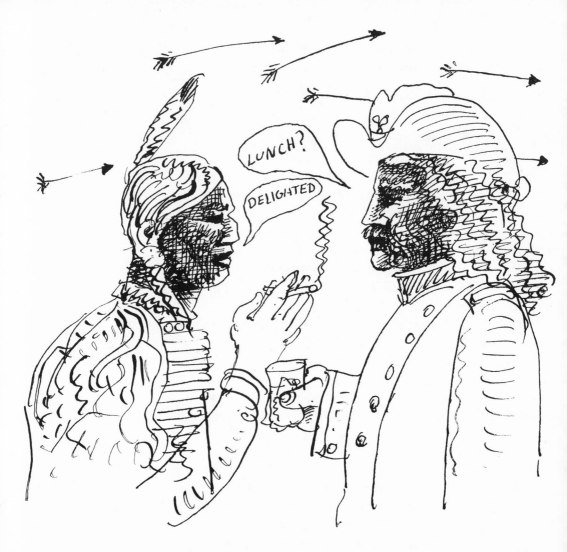

"The first thing is to determine the speaker's sincerity…"

more attractive comes along or need time to check their figures before they have lunch with anyone. Just as "Let's have lunch" may be an evasion, stall or deflection, so, too, may the response.

A smile is the best response. It says nothing. A slight nod accompanying the smile says double nothing. Nobody ever says no.

"I'll call you" is the most common response. This leaves all options open. The alleged call can occur the next day, the next month or when the swallows return to Capistrano.

Timing is important. No one wants to have lunch with people who are too available for lunch. You can't say, "Sure, how about Thursday?" on the spot without appearing to be a wallflower. People who pin the inviter down immediately get cancellation calls in the morning. The custom is to promise to call and say that you have to "consult your calendar." This gives you time to decide whether you want this lunch or not.

The priggish response to "Let's have lunch" is "Sorry, I never do." This surpasses, in its smugness, the renunciations of former alcoholics, heroin addicts and fingernail biters. It is often followed by a litany that sounds like this:

"Oh, I used to go along with the lunch thing. That was back in the days when I was a cog in the

7

social machine. But since I saw the light of not lunching, let me tell you…"

Whereupon follows a list of improvements in their lives since giving up lunch:

"I fly through my paperwork. My breathing's more regular. And my teeth are shinier, have you noticed? I even get more respect from doormen and cleaning ladies."

Masochists react to these remarks by plotting nefarious ways to get nonlunchers to lunch. What the masochists really have in mind is not lunch but publicity. There is a certain cachet in being seen publicly with a known nonluncher, but it is hardly ever worth the effort.

On Refusing Invitations

People who refuse to lunch fall into three categories:

The Controller will go to pieces if he is not in charge of his life and environment. The prospect of walking the streets at midday with all those people weaving about, none marching single file, horrifies him. Refusing to live by other people's time schedules— waiting for a table, waiting for a waiter—he prefers the purified and the arranged. The Controller has nightmares about being asked questions he can't answer (people say the damnedest things at lunch!) or being stuck across the table from someone bent on expressing himself. Left in his office while every-one else lunches, he makes lists headed "Bring Me; Get Me; Show Me" and checks things, like the height of his chair or his eye-blink rate. The Controller may also be a woman.

The Anorexic imagines milk shakes pouring out of the water cooler. She hallucinates chocolate mousse in the ventilating system. Forced to overcome her fear of food and go to lunch, she makes a delightful lunch partner. Otherwise unacceptable mannerisms like table-hopping or leaving lunch to make long telephone calls actually please her. Convinced she will be impaled on artichokes, she hides food in her purse during her partner's absence. When her partner is present, she gives him or her undivided attention. Since it is difficult to be the only one at the table eating, the partner usually returns to the office flattered but hungry. Men have been known to be anorexic from time to time.

The Guiltmonger is the worst kind of lunch refuser. This person says, loudly, clearly and pointedly, that he or she has too much work to do. You are made to feel lazy and irresponsible for asking in the first place. Every office has its guy riding the elevators in shirt-sleeves saying, "Going out to lunch, huh? I can't. I'm snowed under with work." These same people are there when you return from lunch and they always say, "How was it?" dripping with accusation. They may be company shills.

THE MISGUIDED VIRTUES OF LUNCH AT YOUR DESK

esk lunchers begin by clearing a space for lunch. This involves making two stacks of papers with a placemat-size space between them. They never find anything in the stacks of papers again.

The desk luncher dials the take-out service. The line is busy.

He has discovered the strategy of returning phone calls at lunchtime. These calls are from people he doesn't want to talk to. It gets him off the hook, he thinks, to have called back and missed the other party. When he tries to do it, however, he reaches the person he wants to avoid who is also, interestingly, having lunch at his desk that day.

When the take-out service is not busy, he is put on hold while they play "I Did It My Way." He gets someone else's lunch. The coffee is always cold.

People who eat at their desks spend most of their time fantasizing about people who have gone out to lunch. By the time everyone returns from lunch, those at their desks are ready to start a war or a divorce.

CASTING THE LUNCH

*A*n invitation is an invitation, but a refusal is a blow to your calendar. It also shakes your self-esteem, causing you to wonder if you are really as good at casting the lunch as you think you are.

Serious lunch invitations contain, beneath their breeziness, definite ideas about what lunch should be, who should be there and what should happen. In this sense, everyone initiating or refusing a lunch invitation sees himself as the director in his own movie. Some of the more popular lunch casts are:

Duos

More people go to lunch in twos than any other combination. Usually, one person wants something and the other person is in a position to give it.

Clients. A *client* always gets taken to lunch. In fact, the definition of client is "a person with whom you must have lunch." Sometimes the client is also known as *the prospect, the customer* or *the mark.* The intention of lunching with clients is to get them or keep them.

Employer and Employee. The protocol about these lunches is rigid. Superiors invite inferiors. Your boss must invite you and you must invite your secretary. The inferior must accept, even if it means changing another lunch appointment. This is called "noblesse oblige." The purpose of these lunches is often to butter someone up or calm someone down. In some cases, there is no purpose at all, although only one of the partners may know that. People often take their secretaries to lunch when they have run out of people to have lunch with or had their own lunch dates canceled. Bosses take employees to lunch because they have read books about management relations.

Associates and Rivals. These are sometimes the same people.

Friends in Need. The need may be emotional or financial. Sometimes the lunch is offered as a substitute for what the friend really needs. Linguini may be easier to provide than a lover, cannelloni than cash, spaghetti than sympathy. Down-at-the-heels friends may require your credit card more than your presence; in that case, send them to lunch while you stay in the office.

The Unclear Situation. Men and women lunching together may have actual business between them. They may have potential business. Or they may have none. They may not know what they are doing. One or both may pretend to be interested in business but be open to or in pursuit of something else. One or both may pretend to be interested in romance but, in fact, be after a different kind of deal. The possibilities are infinite, and the course of the lunch can change at any moment. Under such conditions, lunching is walking a tightrope. This is the most interesting lunch couple.

The Lunch Marriage. A variation on the unclear situation. This, too, involves men and women together, although other combinations are possible. A Lunch Marriage is a long-standing relationship that takes place entirely at lunchtime. The people involved may have long ago decided not to allow it to move beyond the bounds of lunch. Each lunch, then, is a complete and fulfilling encounter. The pleasures of merely lunching satisfy both people and they may hardly know each other if they happen to meet under other circumstances.

Trios

The threesome is the trickiest lunch to cast. The actual operation of trios reveals why they are so tricky. Two women having lunch with a man arrive, by some act of intuition, together or at nearly the same time. Two men lunching with a woman arrive before the woman does. One kind of conversation goes on among the men, another when the woman arrives. You can always hear the gears shift.

The Cop Act. The Cop Act is the old Good Guy/Bad Guy routine. Two lunchers are partners, the third is

The Cop Act

the "potential" or the "mark." One partner plays hard, the other soft. One is usually the money person, the other a creative type. They alternate. One says everything's wonderful; the other says it's all rot. They go for the potential's weak spot. He likes ballet, the Good Guy gives him ballet. He likes bullets, the Bad Guy gives it to him. One eats heavy; the other has a light meal. The potential is slightly confused, but feels, too, that he is in a place where there is something for everyone. He'll be ready to sign before one of them has downed his Campari and the other sipped his Scotch. Do not shine a blinding light in the potential's eye—it gives the game away.

The Chaperone. Invited along to lunch in the unclear situation, the Chaperone is there not so much to keep anything from happening, but to convince the rest of the restaurant and everyone who will hear about this lunch that nothing is happening. Your lunch partner can help you choose the Chaperone. All that is required in casting this role is that the person be able to sit there through the entire lunch.

Groups

Organizing lunch with a group of people is easier. It often does not matter who is there. People who don't get along with each other get lost in the crowd. People who disagree or have nothing to offer can be ignored. Bores can be left with the bread and butter. Creeps take notes.

You can locate any particular group of lunchers in the corporate hierarchy by observing how much time they spend discussing business. Street-corner brown-baggers talk more about Mets scores and scoring in general than they do about take-overs. People with nonexecutive jobs see lunch as recess, a chance to get away from work. (Executives may, too, but less obviously and with less support from their peers.) When lunch is experienced as recess, it resembles high school: The bosses are jerks, just as the teachers were, the work is a drag and most of what goes on in the office is considered stupid. Anyone who deviates from this group talk is seen as a "grind" and eliminated from lunch.

Group lunching is the great leveler of office life. It often resembles the office party in this as well as other aspects.

Ceremonial Lunches. Someone's thirty-fifth year with the firm or fiftieth birthday brings together everyone whose name has ever appeared on an interoffice envelope. These people often don't know or like each other and are at a loss for what to say, which is why they drink and turn lunch into a floating office party. Many of them wish they were having lunch with executive recruiters, so dismayed are they at the prospect of spending thirty-five years with the firm or reaching their own fiftieth birthdays.

The E Pluribus Unum Group. This is a collection of six subjects and one object. A lunch of this kind takes place before or after a major contract signing and is meant to show the object, the person who signed the contract, what a wonderful team he or she has become associated with. To create the impression that the many are, in fact, one requires a great deal of smiling. This lunch is concluded in private, after the object has departed, when the most senior member of the group says, "I think that went very well, don't you?" The answer is always yes.

Chapter Two

❦ THE ARRANGEMENT ❦

TELEPHONES
WHAT SECRETARIES KNOW
MONDAY OR FRIDAY
NOON OR TWO
THE HIATUS

TELEPHONES

*A*ssuming an invitation seriously extended, the act of casting successfully accomplished and calendars duly consulted, the lunch moves into its second stage: *The Arrangement.*

Ordinary arrangements begin with a call. Often, the principals do not participate. They prefer remaining behind their calendars or stalking the corridors saying "Let's have lunch" to other colleagues also avoiding *their* ringing telephones. When you can't get through to someone to arrange your lunch, that person is "in a meeting," at the end of which they will ask one or more persons in the room to have lunch.

he task of arranging lunch, like most potentially embarrassing things, often falls to the secretary—whose conversation with the secretary on the other end (the "My Girl will call Your Girl" dyad) proceeds along these lines:

"Hello. This is Mr. J's secretary, calling to arrange lunch with Mr. L."

"Just a minute, I'll have a look at his calendar."

During the pause, the secretary pops in to ask Mr. L if he in fact intends to lunch with Mr. J.

"Okay. I've got it. How about Tuesday the third?"

"Three weeks from today? I'll check."

She presses the Hold button and taps her fingers on the desk. "You still there? The third's no good. It's his first day back from London. How about Wednesday, the fourth?"

"We have marketing meetings on Wednesdays. Let's go into the next week."

"Well, I can't read what it says here on Monday.

Jane's something...Oh, yes...Never mind...No, not Monday. Wait a minute. Tuesday's the Javits thing... How about...?"

The arrangement may or may not be concluded, but, in either case, both Mr. J and Mr. L will be annoyed at the extreme unavailability of their secretaries, who seem to spend all their time on the telephone.

It is possible, although uncommon, unfashionable and unreliable, to arrange lunch all by yourself.

MONDAY OR FRIDAY

The day of the week is a delicate matter. The optimum distance between the arranging of lunch and its actual occurrence is ten days. Too soon makes you appear anxious and not busy enough; too far off looks diffident, if not hostile. A far-off lunch date is only possible if you have or pretend to have a trip to Africa or a sales conference in Tahiti in the intervening time.

It is always dazzling to offer to cancel a lunch date for someone. People with empty calendars would be well advised to pretend to cancel dates. Begin by saying, "Well, let me see if I can change..."

It is best not to mention the name of the cancelee, legitimate or fraudulent, lest he or she turn out to be having lunch that day with the very person you are speaking with.

Monday

Monday lunch starts the week and you would choose it for matters that require follow-up, investigation and pursuit. A rotten lunch on Monday can ruin your week; a promising one can get you through the weekend. Monday is the best day for lunching with people about whom you will want to say, on Tuesday, Wednesday or Thursday, "Well, Lattimore said at lunch the other day..."

Tuesday

Tuesday is the same, slightly watered down. Tuesday lunches are, however, more energetic, committed and involved because many people have trouble getting into the swing of things on Monday and only get around to a Monday mood by Tuesday. Workaholics and enthusiasts, however, may take a Tuesday invitation to mean you have something better set for Monday.

Wednesday

Wednesday lunch looks forward and backward. There have been two days in which to acquire the information needed to dazzle, interpret and generally work over the person you have lunch with; there are still two more to mull over, apply or celebrate what happened Wednesday. A good Wednesday lunch can pick up an otherwise dull week; a bad one can ruin you.

Thursday

Thursday is a good lunch to set for people whom you like keeping in a state of eager anticipation. By Thursday, everyone knows who you have lunched with all week and is eager to discover what you are up to. A bad Thursday lunch is not as devastating as a Monday debacle. The week is nearly over.

Friday

Friday is the most open lunch of the week. Friday can be anything. The need to return to the office after lunch lessens; expectations that you will return are nil. Romantic lunches take place on Friday more than any other day. Lunch is longer. A late lunch can be endless. Married people lunching with lovers choose Friday because they stock up on whatever gets them through the weekend. Or that's what they say. Married people with lovers pretend to dread the weekend with the family; they can only get away with this on Friday. It is also an all-around good time for garnering sympathy. You can't hold your head in your hands and complain about how hectic it is or how swamped you are on a Monday, after all.

NOON OR TWO

*L*unch at noon is not lunch at two. The best time for lunch has nothing to do with digestion. A noon lunch doesn't count, has little prestige, unless it involves several people and will clearly go on most of the day. Noon seems dismissive to most people, although this varies from place to place. (In Houston, for example, lunch begins at eleven. Lord knows why.) There is only one sort of person who can make a noon date with aplomb: the Double Luncher. This person does his best and only business at lunch and so does it twice a day. He gets away with it by pretending to the first person that he has an early afternoon plane to catch and to the second that his conference call went on until two.

The conventional time for business lunches has now been set at one o'clock. At one, restaurants are crowded with people who are not in the know, the kind of people who order Jello.

Any time later than one has implications. Two o'clock lunches have a European flavor, which may or may not be desirable. Late lunching makes it clear that you are not a clock puncher. Since few among us can endure the hours between breakfast and late lunch without plummeting blood sugar, late lunchers are also notorious snackers.

THE HIATUS

*L*ogic dictates that all arrangements for lunch could well be concluded once the date and time have been settled. What a fool logic is.

Parkinson's Law points to the extreme pleasure people get in protracting everything about lunch. One could assuredly eat a meal in three minutes, and some do, but such people have assigned lunch to the realm of the unimportant. One might simply down a food capsule or, as nutritionists sometimes suggest, consume several puny meals in the course of a day, but few on earth do.

The fun of lunching is inflation.

Were the participants to settle on a place to eat at this stage of their negotiations, there would be nothing to do on the day of the lunch except go to it. Almost no one behaves this way.

Between the first conversation and the day of the lunch, both serious lunchers prepare, fantasize and announce their upcoming lunch to all who will listen.

Chapter Three

🍎 PREPARATION 🍎

DRESSING
PREPRANDIAL TENSION
NEGOTIATING WHERE TO EAT: LUNCH IS A SPECTATOR SPORT
RESERVATIONS

DRESSING

*P*eople who plan their lunches also plan their clothes. The necessity for planning is often brought home by one bad experience. Wearing jeans to the office and suddenly being invited to the best place in town is one such bad experience. A person so misdressed has four choices: Buy something new to wear, borrow clothes, pass it up or tough it out. Women are more prone to borrowing in such a situation than men are, often borrowing across the board—a blouse here, a necklace there—and consuming the entire morning doing it. The people they have borrowed from are resentful of wearing castoffs to their lunches while their clothes go to the best places. People who buy new clothes for lunch always regret it because the clothes are never what they would have bought in their right minds.

You can dress up or down, depending on what you want to accomplish. Writers planning to beg their editors for additional advance money for their novels do not succeed if they are wearing Adolfo dresses and coats or Saint Laurent ties.

The trouble with dressing for lunch is that it is done early in the morning. Even those who have been meticulous in their planning—having mastered the principles of clothing as both announcement and camouflage, intimidation and invitation, standing out or blending in—are thwarted by life's little quirks. The clothes they want to wear are always at the cleaners. If they have been returned, the pockets are filled with small crumpled material, remnants of something stuffed into them at lunch the week before. If the remnants are recognizable, they turn out to be important business cards, acquired at lunch, now soggy, streaked and pressed.

Underwear

A man may well wear one kind of underwear to lunch with his boss and another kind to lunch with his secretary. A woman may choose different underwear for lunch with a female friend than she would for a male friend. These choices are often unconscious. They have to do more with the way underwear makes you feel than with anything that will actually happen at lunch. Sometimes, however, the choices are related to what happens.

Married people have trouble putting the Naked Lunch Law into practice. Their spouses notice their choice of underwear. A husband may remark: "Where did you get that?" observing a flimsy bit of lingerie hitherto unknown to him. A wife's eye may be caught, in the dim light of the bedroom, by her husband's fire-engine-red bikini and she may think this unusual for a man who has worn white boxer shorts all his life. These courtings of domestic suspicion underscore the need to think ahead about lunch. People trying to slip into appealing underwear without arousing such suspicion take to dressing in the bathroom or dressing in the dark or—inconvenient but safe—stuffing the garment into their briefcases.

Outerwear

A man wearing his best dark suit to the office attracts attention. This is difficult for people who are having lunches with executive recruiters and trying to hide that fact from everyone around them. "Hey, got a big lunch?" someone is bound to say. A woman wearing especially attractive clothes for a big lunch will attract

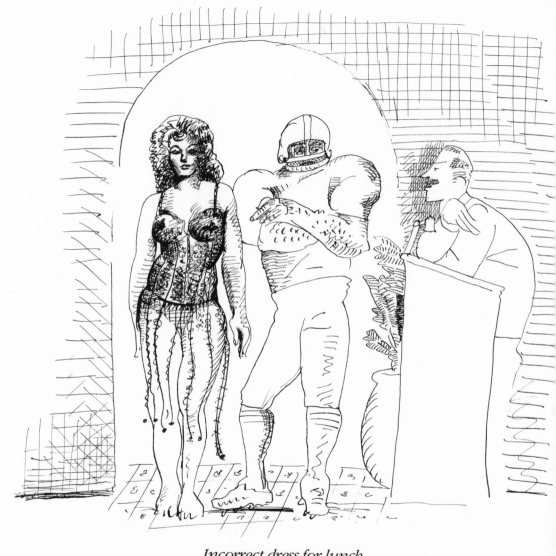

Incorrect dress for lunch

a different kind of attention. People in the office will think she is having an affair.

Men do not worry about appearing too masculine at lunch. It is impossible to appear too masculine, except, perhaps, if you wear a football uniform. Women in business, on the other hand, have learned that clothing considered too feminine works against their business interests, since they are taken less seriously than they want to be. Women button up for lunch.

There is no way around the provocation that special lunch clothing causes in the office except to change clothes before lunch. Clark Kent understood this principle well, although he caught a draft every time he stepped into a handy telephone booth.

PREPRANDIAL TENSION

*L*unch moves closer to actually happening. The morning is spent waiting for the other person to call to make the final confirmation and decide where to eat. The minutes click by. Each person waits for the other to call. This resembles the adolescent game of "chicken." Everybody would rather be called than call. Finally someone gives in.

🍎 PRINCIPLES OF DRESSING

1. Suntans are clothing. You can wear your suntan to any posh restaurant in any major urban area. Ladies are required to wear suntans to all meetings with film executives that take place over lunch in the sight of other people.

2. Captains and maîtres d' are notoriously allergic to polyester. A person wearing polyester to lunch will be sent as far from the captain's nose as possible.

3. If the top of what you wear does not match the bottom of what you wear and you do not work in any of the "creative" fields, it is best to remain seated all through lunch.

4. Writers can wear anything they like. Nobody takes them seriously anyway.

This call occurs on the morning of the lunch so that both parties have adequate time to recheck their schedules, allow for impromptu emergencies or change their minds.

Cancellations

Cancellations on the appointed day require unassailable excuses. Being called out of town or to a meeting at the White House will do. Having indigestion or feeling fat will not do. Broken hearts are no excuse for missing lunches; they are, in fact, a reason for having them. The unforeseen arrival of a carrier pigeon from the Kingdom of Kuwait is a decent excuse for canceling lunch.

A canceled luncher agrees cheerfully to postpone and reschedule the lunch, then falls into paroxysms of despair. He pretends to be relieved, announces to the secretary that this, after all, is a day to be spent catching up on office work, but will usually try to find another lunch date. After all, the luncher has dressed for lunch.

The increasing panic of people left lunchless is heartbreaking to observe. They call emergency standbys only to find everyone out of town, booked for lunch or down with the flu. Then they cruise the office, beginning with the people at their own level, descending to assistants and to secretaries. Their own secretaries are aces in the hole, but sometimes even the ace falls through. In that case, the desperate soul takes the elevator starter to lunch.

NEGOTIATING WHERE TO EAT: LUNCH IS A SPECTATOR SPORT

*I*f, however, the morning call brings confirmation that the lunch is actually on, the parties then negotiate the location of the lunch. Some people do this in advance, but many others enjoy the daredevil thrill of negotiating on the brink. The issues at stake in a location negotiation are:

The Inside Lunch vs. the Outside Lunch and the Danger of Picnics

Some people cling to their offices, others prefer a change of scenery. Someone who hates lunch anyway will, if persuaded, have you come to the office. The company cafeteria or the private dining room are "inside" lunches. An inside luncher has something specific in mind and insists on being in absolute control, although he will hardly confess to it and will, instead, claim to be too busy to get out.

An "outside" lunch is sometimes necessary for a very "inside" reason. People with secret business try to go as far from their offices as they possibly can.

The nether reaches of any city are appropriate for such purposes. Dockhands do not report to their superiors that the man from Acme is "talking" to Boswell.

The most "outside" lunch there is is the picnic, an extremely dangerous form of lunching. Picnics are downright pagan. There are few rules, few utensils and little of the civilizing influence provided by waiters and onlookers. People often eat with their hands at picnics and can sit as close to one another as they choose.

If both people agree to go out for lunch, their suggestions about where to go indicate who they are and what they have in mind. If both agree to a picnic, they deserve each other.

Monogamy vs. Polygamy

Some people have steady places and some lunch around. The ones with steady places are afraid of the rest of the world. These are controllers, re-creating in restaurants or clubs the regularity and security that they insist on in their offices. A steady place is one where the luncher is recognized, called by his or her name, always given the same table. There is usually an artifact on the table to mark it as the luncher's spot. Just as a wedding ring marks the institutionalization of the tie between people, the object on the table marks the luncher's marriage to the restaurant or club. The most common such artifacts are a bottle of Scotch, a special wine or a certain kind of flower.

Equally ritualistic is the monogamous luncher's relationship to the people in the place. Coat check people, waiters and captains say the same thing to them every day: "Good afternoon, Colonel, and how's the war going today?" or "Bonjour, Brooke, you are looking most elegant this afternoon." They know, without being told, that the luncher prefers salad after dessert, club soda in a Martini glass, or martinis in pitchers. Like decent, deferential spouses, they indulge idiosyncratic behavior with nary a question.

The guest of a steady luncher always feels slightly embarrassed, as though he or she has stumbled into someone else's boudoir. The monogamous luncher is often a person with a bad marriage, attempting to substitute stability at lunchtime for the chaos of life at home.

The monogamous luncher sometimes cheats on his restaurant. Occasionally, he allows himself to be persuaded to have lunch elsewhere. On the rare occasion when he initiates eating elsewhere, he is so consumed by guilt that he cannot digest the meal. Often, he is gleeful. He likes fooling around— although he knows he is trading pheasant for scrambled eggs—but he hates the consequences. The return of a wayward luncher to the steady

Naked Lunch Law #2

restaurant is marked by frowns on the captain's face and inquisitive stares from the rest of the staff. The guilt-ridden luncher offers explanations for the previous day's absence without being asked.

My Turf vs. Your Turf

Two inside lunchers or two monogamists do not necessarily find themselves in accord about lunch. Each prefers his own inside, his own regularity.

It is not always apparent that your companion is pushing for his turf. He may simply mention a restaurant. To understand the implication, you must be wise to his or her lunch habits (Is that his steady place?) and the geography of the metropolis (Is that next door to her office?). You need to know the sociology of restaurants. If an advertising person suggests a place where hairdressers eat, there is probably something nefarious afoot. If someone wants to go to a place his boss is known to frequent, something is intended for display, probably you.

A compromise about turf results in people having lunches in places that are impossible to get to, but equidistant from both offices, where the food is rotten and the waiters topless. Compromise always leads to mutual sullenness.

Negotiating in the Unclear Situation

That these negotiations are in code becomes most

🍎 *NAKED LUNCH LAW #2: THE POSSIBILITY OF LUNCH BECOMING EROTIC IS DIRECTLY PROPORTIONAL TO THE DISTANCE FROM THE OFFICE YOU ARE WILLING TO TRAVEL.*

apparent when they are conducted between men and women in the Unclear Situation. In this twilight zone, Sigmund Freud, Dear Abby and Noam Chomsky would be required to interpret what is going on. One partner will suggest a restaurant. The other will reject it on the grounds that it is too noisy. The truth is that it is too close to the office. Another location will be offered. That one will be rejected because one luncher ate there the day before or because it is known to be going downhill. Eventually, one of the partners will catch on. Or will not.

In these, as in all such conversations, the longer the negotiation goes on, the more there is to it.

RESERVATIONS

People make themselves crazy trying to buck the system of tables. They make reservations with Doctor before their names, assuming it has a cachet it does not. The only thing Doctor will get you is a tap on the shoulder if someone has an attack of appendicitis. You can always use a celebrity's name—no one can sue you for not being the *right* Nancy Reagan or the *right* Burt Reynolds. This is not a good trick to pull if you haven't let your lunch partner in on the scheme. "Burt Reynolds?" she will say when you are called, peering behind your back, "where?"

A "good" company name might get you a good table, but the captain may reshuffle when he gets a look at you. A third-party recommendation is sometimes useful—"David Stockman said this is his favorite place to eat in New York"—but it is important to check that the third party is not someone who has recently eloped with a busboy or left an unpaid check on the table.

Some pretentious restaurants have "A" lists and "B" lists for reservations. Unknowns hardly stand a chance in these places and it is as impossible to move from B to A as it was to move from the nerd table to the star table in high school.

Chapter Four

❦ ARRIVING AND POSITIONING ❦

FINDING THE RESTAURANT
WAITING
LATENESS
WALKING TO THE TABLE AND WORKING THE ROOM
TABLES: GOOD AND BAD

FINDING THE RESTAURANT

*F*irst, it is important to find the place you are having lunch in on the right day and at the right time. One illustration of Murphy's Law is the inability of otherwise competent people to locate the restaurant. Next to general befuddlement, insufficient information—"In the Sixties," "In the Mission District," "Near the bridge"— is the most common cause of being unable to find the restaurant. Having the name wrong doesn't help either—the Swedish Pavilion is not the Swiss Chalet, although one

41

partner thinks it is; Tom and Joe's is not Harry and Dick's; and Club 19 is not 21. One of those is usually a strip joint or transvestite bar, the other an elegant restaurant.

In fast-growing urban centers, people are having increasing trouble finding restaurants because they have identified the location by some familiar landmark—"next to the old post office," for example, or "around the corner from the Stock Exchange." They arrive at what they think is the right place only to find the landmark gone. "Oh, yes," a passerby will say, "they used to have a post office here once, but it's been torn down" or "Where you been, man, the Stock Exchange hasn't been in that building for months. Can't you see it's now a powder puff factory?"

Asking someone to meet you at your office and then going out to lunch is a conventional way of avoiding not being able to find the restaurant. People ashamed of their offices use the lobby for the same purpose. People ashamed of their lobbies quit their jobs.

Sending a limo is meant to ensure that your lunch partner will find his or her way to lunch. This naïvely assumes that the limo driver knows how to find the restaurant. The same can be said of taxicab drivers.

WAITING

*A*rriving at the restaurant or club and having someone at the door confirm your reservation is reassuring. You are in the right place at the right time, which, according to Napoleon and Bernard Baruch, is half the battle. The other half is your lunch partner.

The first to arrive has several potential courses of action.

The Lobby

At clubs, the guest is asked to wait in a lobby or waiting room until the member—the "host," as he is called—gets there. This is a very vulnerable position. Everyone else going to lunch must pass through the lobby and can observe you. It is not paranoid to see yourself as an interloper and to become increasingly uncomfortable. The longer you wait, the more suspicious the passersby become. Women suffer this humiliation more than men do, for the fanciest clubs still do not have many, if any, women members. Women are kept waiting, and for them, being eyed suspiciously takes on a different cast. The only ways out of this spot are to form your own club or to meet the host elsewhere. Paris is a good place to meet.

In restaurants, the options are to wait at the bar or take a table. People who wait at the bar are keeping their options open and allowing for a hasty exit. People who take tables are optimists. They also enjoy the flushed apologies of late arrivers.

The Bar

The initial relief of having arrived at the right place soon falls away. Anxiety creeps in when the Significant Other does not appear. This accounts for the amount of alcohol consumed at the bar while waiting. It is always hard to know when the other person is considered late, but a good rule of thumb is that if the people who were there when you arrived are eating lunch or falling asleep on the bar, your partner is late.

The Table

People who choose to wait at the table have something with them to keep them occupied. Otherwise, they would be at the bar. The most common thing to do at the table, aside from worry, is look over a computer report. These neatly folded pages spring to life like a jack-in-the-box and spread over the table and the floor. Trying to gather them is like trying to refold a road map while driving at ninety.

Some people make notes while waiting, which arouses suspicion, causing captains and waiters to think they have a food critic in their midst.

There is no anonymity for the waiting luncher. He or she will have passed, on his way to the table, the steady lunchers and the gossips seated near the entrance. They all wait to see who arrives for lunch. The captain glances over from time to time. If the restaurant has telephones that can be brought to the table, the waiting luncher will surely use one, dialing the weather report when he has run out of other calls to make. Nervousness increases. People drum fingers on tablecloths, are touchy on matters that would otherwise pass unnoticed—an olive instead of an onion in the Gibson for example, or an ex-wife being seated at the next table.

The Fake

The most irritating course of action for the first arriver is to leave the restaurant. People who do this do it because they cannot bear to wait. They walk around the block and then step back into the restaurant. If their companions have still not arrived, they do the same thing again. Captains only tolerate this behavior in very well-known customers. The spectators in the restaurant have watched them come and go and so must hide their laughter when, at last, the luncher manages to arrive after the others and launches into a lengthy apology.

The First Lunch

The hardest lunch to wait for is a first lunch. Since people often do business on the telephone with others whom they have never seen, the first meeting, at lunch, is highly charged and presents special difficulties. It is awkward to ask, "How will I know you?" Few people offer to appear with roses in their teeth for the purpose of recognition. It is possible to do research and have colleagues provide a description, but what often happens is your lunch companion has gained or lost twenty pounds, now parts his hair in the middle, became blonde or turned to dressing like a banker. You assume that if you check in with the captain, the other person will find you. Often, they do not. It is not uncommon to find yourselves waiting for one another at separate tables.

LATENESS

A person is considered late when whoever is waiting for him has finished one drink. Fussbudgets set the time slightly earlier. Hang-loose Californians consider you late for lunch if you arrive while the sun is going down and the tables are being set for dinner.

Someone arriving late sees immediately that she has traded impact for position. She is forced to sit on the outside of the banquette or the wrong side of the table. With her back to the room, she won't be able to see what is going on. Forced to give you her absolute attention, she suffers the indignities of getting

Late for lunch

knocked about by waiters, busboys and people table-hopping or on their way to the bathroom.

Andre Malraux said, "The best excuse for being late is to say you took a taxi." Others are, "It's a madhouse. I couldn't get out." "I got tied up with a long-distance call." "I was with Kissinger." You can also say you have been with Lauren Bacall or Reggie Jackson or all three. The person waiting is meant to feel flattered to have in his presence, even if he has waited for an hour, someone so recently in the presence of Kissinger, Bacall or Jackson.

Good friends who have demanded lunch because of a terrible crisis in their lives can only excuse lateness by saying they considered suicide instead of lunch.

Being Stood Up

It is possible for no one to show up. This happens when the other person fails to find the restaurant, has you down for Tuesday, fell asleep or fell in love. The poor luncher who begins to suspect that the other person might not show up gets jumpy and thinks about the telephone.

Telephoning means leaving the lobby, bar or table where you are waiting. The luncher must weigh risk against gain and determine whether the other person will arrrive in his absence, see no one and leave. The walk to the telephone, in this situation, is called approach-retreat.

No one has the right change for the phone; credit cards do not work on local calls; operators give you a lot of flack for using quarters and you cannot reverse the charges.

The first call is to your own office to check with your secretary that you do in fact have the appointment you think you have. Of course, your secretary is out to lunch and you have to hunt up someone else capable of checking your calendar. This takes some time.

Overanxious people return to the lobby, bar or table to see if the other person has arrived. If not, it's back to the phone, fiddling with it, deciding whether to call the office of the person they are waiting for. Unfortunately, they cannot remember that number nor can they bear calling their own offices again to get it.

Half the people waiting do not make this call. Half of those who begin to make it dial the number and hang up.

Each man and woman has his or her point of no return. Women have a shorter point, perhaps because women are generally shorter. Whatever the reason, women often flip their business cards at the waiter, say, "Tell him I waited half an hour," when it was, in fact, ten minutes, and walk out.

Bereavement

One of the saddest things in modern life is walking

the streets after you have been stood up. People in twos and threes are coming and going from lunch. You pick up a sandwich on the way to the office and find your secretary still out to lunch when you get there.

Most lunches take a happier turn.

WALKING TO THE TABLE AND WORKING THE ROOM

*W*hether you arrive first, last or in between, you will make the journey from the entrance to the captain's station and across the room to your table. There are as many ways to do this as there are people lunching, but all manners of crossing the room fall into two categories: the straight and the crooked.

A straight walk to your table gives the appearance of directness. It is often hasty. One sees the beeline walk when someone is late for lunch. It can appear arrogant. Often, people who follow the captain or waiter closely and proceed immediately to their tables are not ignoring the others in the restaurant, although they appear to be, but are nearsighted. People carrying large packages that they refuse to deposit in the cloakroom also go straight to their tables.

The crooked walk is more common. Done quickly, it is quite frenetic; done slowly, it is called meandering. The person crossing the room in this manner looks from side to side, taking in the other lunchers, smiling, nodding and sometimes stopping. When a luncher makes a table stop, he or she is not only being gracious and keeping up contacts, but acquiring information. By the time he reaches his own table, he will know who is in the restaurant, what they are eating and, if he is a fast observer, what they are doing. Thus, he will have something with which to begin his conversation when he sits down.

People walk more slowly to their tables when they are having lunch with an especially attractive member of the opposite sex or with a celebrity. This is a display walk. They also walk slowly to their steady tables in their steady restaurants and even more slowly when lunching at their clubs. This is simply an indication of ease and familiarity.

TABLES: GOOD AND BAD

estaurants are organized on a need-to-know basis. People seated up front get to watch everyone arriving for lunch and are, in turn, watched. This

is called prominence. If there is more than one level to the restaurant, the lower level, provided it is not the cellar, is the most prestigious because it is easier for spectators to gaze down upon the luncher than it is to look up.

The discreet table is just as good as the display table. This is removed from the front of the house, tucked, usually, in a comfortable corner, but close to the captain. Another aspect of prominence is the ability to command quality service by a gesture no larger than a lifted eyebrow.

Everyone wants a good table. Those who get them are those who usually have them. Neither mouthwash nor designer clothes influence the captain to provide a good table if he doesn't think you deserve one.

Bad tables are near doors leading to the kitchen or in a "pit" uncomfortably close to other lunchers. These tables are bad because they force you to hear things in the kitchen you would rather avoid—"Get your fingers out of the ratatouille"—or a conversation exactly like your own at the next table.

Round, Square and Tandem:
The Shape of Things to Come

The shape of the table influences the lunch.

Round tables establish a friendly atmosphere. They are nonhierarchical, although King Arthur found a way to establish his authority in spite of that. Sometimes the pedestal supporting a round table makes it difficult to play footsie under the table or causes you to catch the wrong toe if there are many toes scattered around.

Square tables have clear sides and are thus useful for playing games. The ability to look your opponent squarely in the eye is useful at lunch. Judas's betrayal of Jesus might have been easier to predict if they had been sitting at opposite sides of the table.

Banquettes have become extremely fashionable. Since both lunchers are forced to face the room, this arrangement underscores lunch as a spectator sport. It is difficult, seated beside your lunch companion, to eat and talk at the same time. Banquettes are appropriate to gangsters, however, who speak well out of the sides of their mouths. Although it may prove convenient to be seated beside your companion as he or she looks over the catalog, contract or computer sheet, you almost always leave a banquette lunch with a pain in the neck.

Chapter Five

🍎 TABLE TALK 🍎

OPENERS

People begin talking immediately upon sitting down to lunch. If they don't arrive at the table with news of the room, they launch the conversation with an observation about the other person's appearance. Men who know each other well trade insults on this score as a gesture of affection:

"I like that suit. I've liked it for the last twenty years."

"Put on a few pounds, haven't you, Smith?"

Women compliment each other:

"Hey, you look terrific."

"Oh, come on. My hair's falling out, I have a shiner on my eye and I've developed midlife acne."

"No, really, you look terrific."

From there, people pass on to comments about the restaurant:

"I haven't been here in months because last time the liver walked off the plate."

Restaurants are always, to judge from the conversation, like San Francisco trolleys:

"This place must be going uphill. Jackson's been in twice this week."

"I've been waiting fifteen minutes for the waiter to take my drink order. Since Clarabella took it over it's gone downhill."

DRINKING

*I*n the Old Days, people simply drank at lunchtime and said nary a word about it. Waiters complained that the four-martini lunch kept them from setting up for dinner, but otherwise drinking was simply drinking. Now, purified by winds traveling West to East, fewer people drink and more people talk about it: martini drinkers converted to club soda explain why

Campari-and-soda drinkers lecture the table on the evils of hard liquor, and Perrier nuts announce their orders with pride. People treat Perrier drinkers the way thirty-year-olds and potheads were treated in the sixties.

SMOKING

Smoking, like drinking, does not pass unnoticed. Smokers are defensive, anticipating scorn as they draw cigarettes from their pockets, look apprehensively across the table and light up. They announce how much they have cut down. Their cigarettes are low in tar and nicotine and give them hernias when they inhale. There is nothing more excruciating than a smoker lunching with an ex-smoker who has not quite kicked the habit, drooling and sucking on his fingers.

ALERTNESS: USING ALL YOUR FACULTIES

At the start of lunch, the participants are keyed up. They feel full of possibility: Anything can happen. They also feel relatively equal, which may change in the course of the lunch. But at the beginning, revved up, lunchers are immensely alert.

A man may observe his lunch partner wearing a new suede jacket, remember his years lunching with that fellow in more conservative dress, and open a discussion about extramarital affairs. A woman may observe her partner's new mink coat draped on the back of the chair and ask advice about tax shelters.

Peripheral vision operates acutely at this stage. The lunchers will be aware, without turning their heads, that a new face has appeared at the front booth to join the agent who eats there every day.

Hearing operates with amazing acuity. People who don't hear you talking to them *do* hear what is said on the other side of the room during lunch. The conversation at other tables, it appears, is conducted entirely in nouns. The most frequently overheard nouns at lunchtime are *numbers, equity* and *divorce*.

In the first stage of lunch everyone expects and delivers high levels of performance. Only Woody Allen gets away with sullen lunching.

JOKES

*G*ood joke-telling requires both practice and research. The unfortunate lot of playing audience to someone practicing jokes for lunch falls to families and people in the firm. All joke-tellers have "sources." These are usually people they call on the telephone and do not take to lunch.

Several cities have recorded jokes that you can hear over the telephone. That line is always jammed at noon. If you dial the wrong number and get recorded horoscopes, you will be at a loss for a good part of lunch, unless someone at the table is very interested in the fate of Virgos or why Sagittarians should have stayed in bed that day.

Practicing jokes and collecting them often back-fires. Sometimes, two people come to lunch with the same joke, or someone tells you a joke you told the last time you lunched together or that you told someone else last week. The choice of whether or not to laugh is yours.

The jokes at the table are a good barometer of what is going on in the world. Arab jokes disap-peared as the price of oil rose. Polish jokes stopped when Poles started telling them. For many years, a favorite subject of joking was the sexual inadequacy of Jewish women. Recently, these jokes have been re-placed by jokes about the sexual inadequacy of Jewish men. At the very least, this indicates that there are more Jewish women lunching than ever before.

In groups, the jokes come later. Although ner-vousness makes people want to jump in and start joking, they are always aware of the hierarchy at the

🍎 *IT IS IMPOSSIBLE TO EAT LUNCH WITH YOUR FOOT IN YOUR MOUTH.*

table, afraid of telling the boss's favorite joke or one that he does not think funny. Therefore, the only person permitted to tell the first joke is the person paying the check.

MANTALK/SPORTSTALK

*M*en talk to each other about sports, whether they are interested in the subject or not. Monday and Friday lunches have more sportstalk than other days of the week, since most men who care participate in or watch sports on weekends. A Monday conversation begins like this:

"Had a great tennis game yesterday. Went ten sets."

or:

"I must have smashed my wrist at the net. Does it look swollen to you? That guy's got a cross-court like a cannonball."

Complaints are answered by complaints:

"I pulled a muscle doing my nine miles this morning."

As the men get older, this talk becomes less participatory:

"Do you believe the Giants?"

"Man, Connors is finished."

"You think the Rams are gonna choke again?"
"Who ya got in the Bowl?"

Guide to Sportchat

For everyone intimidated or bored by sports but eager to enjoy lunch, here is a brief guide to the sports seasons and what you might say about them:

Winter. If it is cold outside, you can talk about football. Someone will surprise you and talk about football in August and he won't be wrong, but it is better to be conservative and talk football in cold months. Remember that the play-offs come before the Super Bowl.

Spring. Just mention the Stanley Cup. Remember to take Stanley to lunch.

Summer. Baseball. Somebody is hitting over .400— find out who. Have a position on the designated hitter rule. To acquire one, listen to the guys in the office talking about it at lunch and if that fails, go to the mail room and ask.

Fall. Complain about what is happening to tennis. Smile knowingly about the basketball scandal, perhaps referring to basketball in your college days. Anyone you get World Series tickets for will take you to lunch the rest of the year.

Small Talk

*W*omen talking about clothes or relationships sound like men talking about sports: "They're great suits, but the price is going to put me in hock for the rest of the year."

"Can you believe he still can't make his own coffee?"

Whether it is a garment or a guy. the cost is always too high. Women support one another in these complaints, whereas they only smirk if there are men at the table talking about pulled muscles and swollen wrists.

These, too, are more intense subjects of conversation on Mondays and Fridays, diminishing during the week unless there is a crisis in either category:

"Those black Armani pants I was going to wear this weekend are too tight. Can you give me the Scarsdale diet again?"

"He changed our Friday dinner to Monday lunch. What do you think is going on?"

Guide to Female Small Talk

Although seasons change, the subjects of female small talk remain consistent. For those who enjoy lunching with women and would like to participate more heartily, here is a brief chart of the most common topics that arise at lunch:

Mothers. Anyone who takes the mother's part in a conflict described by a woman at lunch will not be invited a second time.

Weight. All information is meant to be shared. If a woman complains about gaining weight, you must offer to take her to your exercise class and to hand over all diet information in your possession.

Stores. If you ask your lunch companion where she got the blouse she is wearing and she answers, "the Saint Laurent boutique," you are not allowed to scowl.

Men. If you discover a man in common and she lost him, he must be described as a rotten egg. If you are married to him, pray she does not find out. Or complain about him anyway.

Money.

GOSSIP

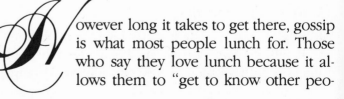 owever long it takes to get there, gossip is what most people lunch for. Those who say they love lunch because it allows them to "get to know other peo-

ple" really mean they love gossip. The rapidity with which one reaches this stage depends on the level of acquaintance with the person across the table. It is not civilized to ask someone your boss asked you to take to lunch who is doing what to whom or whether his company is about to be sold.

There are two kinds of gossip: sexual gossip and industry gossip. The distinction between them is hard to discern and not very important. What counts is the passing of information, any information. This goes directly to the heart of why people lunch: They want to know what is happening. Or, more accurately, they want to feel that they know what is happening. The possession of information is more valuable than its accuracy.

Lunch hardly sits right if you come away from it with nothing but a full stomach.

Other People's Gossip

A consummate luncher attends to the gossip not only at his or her own table but at as many tables as he or she can tune in to. Access to talk at other tables is the only compensation for being seated close to other lunchers. Since one indication of prestige is privacy, there is an interesting relationship here between gossip and rank.

The coffee shop and the brown-bag lunch on the street afford far more opportunity to listen to other people than do the private booth or the executive dining room. The higher you go, then, the less dense the gossip. This is one reason for the alleged loneliness of people at the top.

It ought to be pointed out, however, that the less dense gossip at the top is also more valuable. One assumes that people at the top know more. In fact, how much they know is often related to their ability to delegate the collection of gossip to those below them. The minions are munching for someone. They will use what they overhear to make themselves more valuable within their own hierarchies. There you have one reason for the existence of expense accounts.

Your Own Gossip

Since gossip is lunch's prime commodity, the most important thing to do with it is pretend to have it. This involves nodding your head knowingly when you hear something that blows the pants off you or blows the lid off what you have been sitting on. Gossip is contagious, like hiccups and jokes. If you tell people you have a cold, they tell you about their backaches. If they say "too bad," you stop talking. The same is true of gossip. The only way to keep it going is to respond. Overreacting kills the rhythm.

The least appropriate response to gossip is to jump up, knock the wineglass over and dash to the telephone shouting "Holy Cow!"

"I heard" is the most common form of introducing a piece of gossip. "I heard Al Haig discuss this at lunch last week" may well mean that the speaker was in a room of more than twelve hundred people picking at rubber chickens while Mr. Haig addressed the crowd. You, however, are meant to hear the tidbit as an intimate revelation—Haig to him, him to you. Journalists and politicians are notorious for pretending to have been the only person present when something important was said.

The Four Varieties of Gossip

1. *The Dirty Little Secret.* The DLS is usually preceded by a caveat: "I'm not sure I should tell you this, but..." or "Listen, this can't go beyond this table." The more somber the introduction, the more likely it is that you already know it.

2. *The Badmouth.* Saying nasty things about other people increases with the degree of intimacy among lunch partners. People who work in the same office together or lunch together regularly are more likely to put down the people they know in common than strangers are. Strangers are wisely afraid that the person they badmouth today will be someone they have to ask for a job tomorrow.

3. *The Plant.* The value of anything increases in relation to the amount of time people spend talking about it. You can create a run on novels about one-legged orphans or red sectional Naugahyde couches simply by talking about them at all your lunches. It helps to say that you are finding them hard to get your hands on and to associate Big Names with it. If Calvin Klein loves to read them or Burt Reynolds is now sitting on them, people will follow along. This requires discretion, though, because some Big Names are the Kiss of Death and others are the Midas Touch. If Mark Spitz wants to make a movie of it or Billy Carter can't part from his, the plant won't work.

4. *Rebound Gossip.* Something you told someone else at lunch that week comes back at you. The information has been mangled and you have become the bad guy or the loser in the story.

Gossip Revealed

It is interesting to note how often gossip is described in metaphors of food. "A tidbit," "a morsel," something "juicy." This simply points to the fact that gossip is meant to be consumed. Gossip, then, is like fish, pleasurable today, rotten tomorrow.

This explains why people have to go out to lunch every day.

Chapter Six

🍎 THE MEAL 🍎

FOOD: EMBRACED OR DISDAINED
MENUS
DISCUSSING WHAT TO EAT
THE RETURN OF FOOD
ORDERING
WINE: SHALL WE DANCE?
THE DEAD SPOT
THE ART OF SERVING
EATING

FOOD: EMBRACED OR DISDAINED

Some people actually go to lunch to eat. Two such people discussing where to eat are more interested in the menu than the milieu:

"Where's that great fettucini place you told me about?"

"I gotta have Chinese food today or I'll pass out."

"I haven't had a good goose in a long time."

The moment the menu arrives feels like the night before Christmas to

69

food lovers. Actually, the menu is redundant, for they have eaten the meal in their imaginations long before they arrived at the restaurant.

Food lovers do not enjoy lunching with food disdainers. These are people who find food an irritating distraction and have to be seduced into paying attention to it. Food disdainers have or pretend to have "bigger things" on their minds.

MENUS

*F*ood is announced in one of two media: print or live performance. There is all the difference in the world between them.

Written

Reaction to a menu, as to all print media, is entirely in your control. If the menu arrives as you are praising someone's elbows or boasting about your product, you can ignore it. A menu does not talk back.

Menus are often constructed in ascending order of price. If you have a short attention span, you will have a cheap meal.

Some menus read like novellas or tasteless

newspapers, with the words *tantalizing* or *sensational* appearing every third line. A good rule of thumb for reading menus is, the tastiness of the dish is inversely proportional to the length of its description on the menu.

Reading the menu is a mutual mediation done in silence, punctuated by comments like:

"I hear the pastry chef was so devastated by his lover's sex change operation that he just can't flake it like he used to. I'd skip the Beef Wellington."

"Where would they be getting it now that we've stopped trade with Iran?" Or China. Or Cuba. Caviar, truffles and, later, cigars, lend themselves to this sort of comment. It shows the profundity with which the international situation hits where it hurts.

"I've had so much fish lately, I'm growing gills." There is no appropriate response to this particular comment.

Oral

The oral announcement of the food differs from the menu in that you must pay attention to it. The waiter, captain or owner of the restaurant recites at your table. He cannot be interrupted. If you ask a question, he will begin again, from the beginning. His descriptions are as florid or lurid as those on the printed menu and sometimes have accompanying illustrations. If the owner appears with pad and pen in hand

and proceeds to illustrate his narration with drawings, they look like the Dallas Cowboys' game plans.

Many recitals of available food are censored. Announcers tell you only what they think you should consider eating. Or they omit certain dishes, like the cottage fries they are saving for their best customers. These mental processes are impossible to fathom because they are often irrational or have to do with management-labor tensions of which the poor luncher is ignorant.

DISCUSSING WHAT TO EAT

The twin purposes of discussing *what* to eat with your companion are to show off how much you know about food and to find out who is going to pay for the meal.

Showing off involves comparison. You can consider the cheeseburger aloud and dismiss it because no cheeseburgers measure up to the ones you had just outside Des Moines or on the Champs-Elysees. This place may use too much tarragon in the liver, but Guido's does it just right. Sauces and spices are excellent subjects for pretentious talk. You can sneer at the stock anywhere except Wall Street.

Whoever asks "What are you having?" is usually in control of the lunch.

Between the Chef's Salad and the Steak

Discussing whether you will have the salad or the steak, the quiche or the venison, just soup or a five-course meal is an attempt to find out who will pick up the check and how large a tab is acceptable. A smart luncher will pretend not to be able to decide. His or her partner then has the option of saying, "Oh, the steak here is superb." When the partner is clearly buying lunch, this is less an evaluation of the food than permission for the luncher to have an expensive meal.

A light meal is sometimes chosen for reasons that are not financial. It is perfectly acceptable for fat people to eat lightly because everyone assumes they are dieting. Thin people doing the same are taken to be self-effacing and always evoke comments urging them to eat. People with "great things" on their minds choose light meals in order not to clog their brains.

The most expensive thing on the menu is not necessarily the best thing, although lunchers on the take don't know it. These gold diggers often order a full five-course meal, forcing everyone else to overeat or drum on the table much of the time. Such behavior does not encourage goodwill or return engagements.

Struggling painters, principled poets and down-at-the-heels gigolos will order the heavy meal because it is their only meal of the day, perhaps the only decent meal of the week. If you are not prepared to indulge them, you ought not to have invited them to lunch. Many people in business do, however, set aside some lunches for their friends the painters, poets and gigolos.

A large meal ordered by your partner is a bad sign if you hope the lunch will take an erotic turn. Alas, large meals dull the senses and make people tired. On the other hand, some potential romantics order large meals and are unable to eat them. That is a good sign. Wine, of course, makes people more receptive, particularly if a lot of wine gets consumed while the food is being ignored.

THE RETURN OF FOOD

We have gone through several predictable cycles of the lunch-as-an-indication-of-prosperity. For several years, the general attitude has been that less is more. Merely picking indicated a great reservoir of power. The Power of Positive Picking, it was called, and it went along with Perrier addiction.

Now, however, there are hints that food is making a comeback. People are bored with butterless sauces. Heartiness is returning to the lunch table. The trouble is, everyone has got used to being thin. How to manage aligning yourself with the new expansiveness without actually expanding?

For some reason, only stockbrokers and lawyers have figured this out. They skip dinner. This does cause marital discord, for people who eat large lunches and skip dinner often live with spouses who go light on lunch and want a significant family meal at the end of the day. Life is difficult.

Our Kind of Food

The kind of food you choose identifies you in several ways to your lunch companions. Some people have "the usual" food, just as they have "the usual" restaurant, table or drink. Legendary captains of industry who command people's presence in their private dining rooms every lunchtime, oddly enough, do not dazzle their own or anyone else's palate with glamorous food, but shock instead by insisting on banal meals—tuna fish, cheeseburgers and egg salad day after day. People who order "the usual" or manage to indicate that they are eating today what they had yesterday give the impression of both reliability and cowardice. People who go from tortellini one day to club sandwiches the next to blintzes after that are

Our kind of food

cosmopolitan and adventuresome, but are sometimes seen as lacking definition and too easily shifted
by the winds of taste.

More importantly, everyone makes a judgment
about "our kind of food." An otherwise congenial
lunch can be disrupted by a food order that curls the
nostrils of the others at the table. Childish as these
leftover cultural attitudes may be, they are immensely
operative. Many a corporate climber has been felled
by a predilection for pastrami.

Some of the more provocative foods are:

Macaroni and Cheese. Fast becoming the food of
presidents, macaroni and cheese, along with Welsh
rarebit and chicken hash, are WASP soul foods. They
are often served in clubs. Those whose taste runs to
the more pungent find these dishes impossibly
bland. Continentals object to the color. Some people
persist in thinking of these dishes as "goo."

Herring. This is the other side of the coin, one of
several Jewish soul foods, most of them delicatessen
foods like pastrami, borscht and chopped liver. The
pungency of these foods leads some conservative
lunchers to identify them with loud voices and
attention-getting clothes.

Garlic. Many lunchers are afraid of garlic. Although a
sophisticated restaurant owner would look down his
supercilious nose at these timid souls, they have

history on their side. Egyptian priests banned garlic as an "unclean abomination," because it stimulated the digestive system. People seeking to avoid stimulation of any kind steel themselves when someone at the table orders oysters or truffles, for the same reason. These are alleged aphrodisiacs.

Escargots. Snails make some lunchers jumpy. People are wary of foods that are tricky to eat and shy away from them when they feel on display. The same people are equally unnerved by foods that are hard to pronounce or that they fear pronouncing wrongly. This category finds "borscht," reappearing, sitting beside snails for perhaps the first time in culinary history.

ORDERING

*I*n restaurants, someone has to speak to the waiter. In clubs, no one does. Club meals are usually ordered by the "host" and written on a pad at the beginning of the meal. This eliminates having to speak to anyone and also diminishes spontaneity. If the drinks have gone well and you decide to have a go at the escargots after all, it will be difficult to accomplish. It is equally difficult to speak to the waiter, for waiters have a rhythm of their own. They come to take your order when you are in the middle of a sentence or do not come when you are ready to order, have created a pause in the lunch and are looking for them.

Ordering first is like going through a door first. You never know what is on the other side. If the discussion of what to eat has not been conclusive, you take your lunch in your hands when you order first. The other lunchers either fall in line behind the first order or go to opposite sides of the menu.

Mom's Lunch

In spite of their protests, some people actually like to be ordered for. It reminds them of childhood, the glee of coming home to tuna on the table, the security of sensing a firm and steady hand behind the peanut butter in the lunch box. If you order for someone else, you become mother. Mothering has certain advantages: It gives you command of the situation, it shows you are easy with authority and definite about decisions—it also exposes you to all of Mom's hazards, particularly to being blamed if the meal goes badly.

*S*hall we have wine? is a loaded question. It sounds like "Shall we dance?" and is often taken that way. Although men lunching together and women lunching together do drink wine, it appears most frequently in Unclear Situation lunches, where the answer is preceded by a thoughtful pause, and at celebratory group lunches, where it turns the lunch into an office Christmas party.

Choosing Wine: Strawberry or Vanilla?

Studying the wine list is not like studying the menu because only one list is brought to the table. The person reading the wine list is the person whose lunch it is, whatever may happen later. The wine list reader may or may not consult the other lunchers about the choice of wine. Often, this person simply mutters to him- or herself, loud enough for the others to hear:

"Let me see. The Pouilly-Fumé was too flinty last time. Ah, if they only had a '76 instead of a '77."

Wine experts, like joke-tellers, study. They not only have hot lines to people who know, but sometimes carry crib sheets, small cards indicating the best vintage for selected wines. They may try to get a look at these cards without anyone catching them at it. Sometimes they do this in the rest room.

There are two categories of choice facing the wine orderer. One is, domestic or imported? This is a very good subject for conversation and, if the lunchers have nothing else to talk about, could well consume the rest of the lunch. It is possible to use the choice of wine to discover your companions' politics or to make a speech about your own. In some quarters, you can be judged a patriot or a traitor depending on whether the wines you like come from the Napa Valley or the Loire.

The second category of choice is simply, strawberry or vanilla?

Ordering the Wine

The hardest thing to do, once the wine has been chosen, is convey that choice to someone who can implement it. Whether it be waiter, captain, wine steward or owner, he will stand at your table staring into the middle distance and you will say to him, confidently:

"We'll have the Châteauneuf-du-Pape, please."

He will furrow his brow and browse over your shoulder at the wine list, where each wine comes with a number as well as a name. "Excuse me?" he will say uncomprehendingly and you will, reluctantly, point to the Châteauneuf. He will smile with recognition: "Ah, number forty-seven!"

If, on the other hand, you act as though you

were in a delicatessen and order by number—"Bring us number forty-seven, please"—he will scowl, look down at the wine list and pointedly pronounce the name of the wine.

THE DEAD SPOT

The lunchers are left alone. After all that activity, it is difficult simply to sit there feeling either hungry or nervous. They eavesdrop and look around the restaurant less energetically than before. One or the other will wish, briefly, that he or she were elsewhere.

For lack of anything else to say, someone may refer to the ostensible purpose of the lunch. This will be done gently, with the expectation that any moment the food will arrive. In groups, small talk runs out fast, unless everyone is drinking and celebrating a deal. Therefore, the purpose of the lunch will be floated and the duration of the float will depend on how many people are present.

Bad lunchers blurt out everything at this point, ruining all appetites at the table. Good lunchers are consummate floaters. Romantics float romance and sometimes immediately leave the restaurant. They usually get billed for the meal anyway.

THE ART OF SERVING

*T*he food arrives while one of you has left the table to go to the rest room or to shake hands all around the room.

or:

The food arrives as you reach the punch line of a joke.

or:

You are telling a saucy story and the waiter puts the food on the table as the least attractive word in the story escapes your lips. He looks shocked and disapproving.

or:

The waiter appears as you have let yourself go in grief over a lost love or a lost job and tears have started falling onto the tablecloth.

EATING

*F*ood lovers greet the arrival of the food with relief, for they have held their appetites in check for so long that it hurts. Gourmands are always disappointed, for few meals live up to their fantasies. Still, their eyes

✿ MURPHY REAPPEARS

1. The waiter returns to say they are out of what you ordered.
2. The person at the next table has the last of what you ordered and you must watch him eat it as you fiddle with your second choice.
3. The wine is not available. You cannot pronounce any other wine on the list.
4. Your lunch partner indicates, in a very offhand way, a distinct lack of interest in what you plan to bring up later. You lose your appetite.
5. Your ex-spouse is seated at the next table.
6. Your lunch companion reveals plans to marry your ex-spouse or close a deal with your competitor.

caress the pheasant the way the soldier in war movies looks at the girl he's come back to after all those years.

In high-powered business lunches, the food is a cease-fire and a resting place. People take their elbows off the tables. Conversation slackens somewhat, although table manners are conspicuously on display.

At recruiting lunches, the recruit is always asked a question when he or she has a mouthful of food. There are usually several polite questioners at these lunches, each eating at a different moment. The recruit, if responsive, is the last to finish the meal. He *doesn't* say, "Wait till I get this crab down, will ya?"

Ladies engaged in "le grand shopping lunch" are appalled by the arrival of the food and stare at the waiter with annoyance.

How to Eat the Food

Eating is difficult with so much going on, but some people manage. What was floated is still in the air and all lunchers lifting fork to mouth are trying to decipher what was just said. The first fork lifter is the one least concerned with the business or the most secure or the most hungry.

At times, it is hard to know how to eat what has been served. This is particularly true at large group lunches or meals your companion has ordered for you. These usually begin with dishes that do not appear in their original form, like a pineapple that has been taken apart, filled with a conglomeration of other things and put back together again. One touch of the fork and it falls into your lap.

Dishes that arrive with special eating tools that you have never seen before are trouble. Watching other people does not help; they all appear to be masters of sleight of hand.

The tiny things atop the food are probably edible. This does not apply to toothpicks.

If a restaurant is famous for its sauces, you may be surprised to discover nearly nothing at all beneath the sauce. This is not a mistake. It is haute cuisine.

The Rhythm of Eating

If the lunch is going well, the lunchers eat at synchronized speeds. There is nothing more disconcerting to the average luncher than discovering that her lunch partner is a picker or a gorger. A picker evokes guilt in the other luncher. A picker, who appears too lost in "big thoughts" to actually eat the food, causes everyone else at the table to feel mundane. Gorgers, on the other hand, make everyone feel repressed, tight-assed and tight-lipped.

The act of tasting one another's food is considered a compliment in some circles and a barbarism in others. "Would you like some?" said as the meal

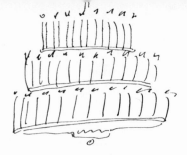

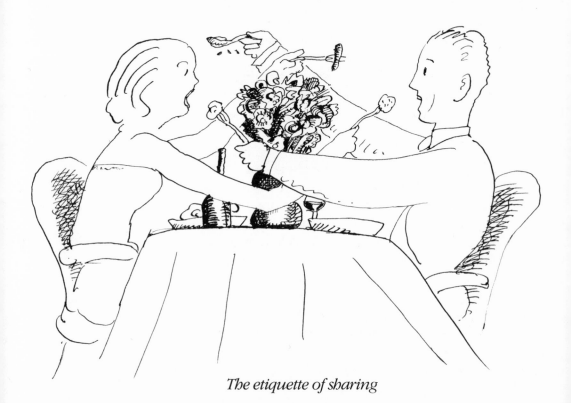

The etiquette of sharing

gets under way, refers to this ritual. The food is either placed on one's own fork and set gingerly on the plate of the other luncher, or if the people know one another well, each stabs at the other's dish. Lovers do this more than business acquaintances. In the Unclear Situation, it may or may not be a sign of further intimacy to come.

Some people sink into the meal and are not heard from until the plates are cleared. Some are so distracted by the conversation that they drop the food into their laps. Neophyte lunchers who don't realize they are meant to cease and desist for the course of the meal blatantly continue to press the business. These compulsive talkers ignore the crucial moment when the owner or manager reappears.

Checking Up

The owner or manager checks up on the course of the meal by asking: "How is everything? All right? Yes?" He nods and smiles, has answered in advance. It is difficult to say anything is wrong. If you do, he will find something wrong with you. Anyone who sends a dish back will not only incur the wrath of the manager, but will take half an hour longer to finish his meal, thereby incurring the wrath of his lunch companions as well.

🍎 GASTRIC DISTRESS

The three most common reasons for gastric distress as the meal continues are:
1. The relentless pursuit of business by someone at the table.
2. The sinking feeling that it is not going well; that you will not get the order or not get seduced; that you are boring your lunch partner; that you are about to be fired.
3. Erotic tension. This is the most pleasant kind of gastric distress.

Gearing Up

For most of the meal, the lunchers participate in the spirit of camaraderie and goodwill that surrounds people who break bread together—the ancient ritual that led such great lunchers as Sitting Bull or Don Corleone to insist on group eating as a peace-making device. This, however, begins to fade as the meal approaches its end. The ostensible equilibrium of the lunch is about to be disrupted. Everyone knows it. Throughout the apparently peaceful interlude of eating, they, like Sitting Bull and Don Corleone, have been gearing up for the next big moment.

Chapter Seven

🍎 DENOUEMENT: THE MAIN EVENT 🍎

ENTRE LE POIRE ET LE FROMAGE
THE PITCH
THE MATINEE: SPONTANEOUS DESSERT
THE MOROSE COURSE

ENTRE LE POIRE ET LE FROMAGE

he French know a great deal about the rhythm of lunch. In fact, they know so much about it that they have an exact phrase for the precise moment when the business of the lunch makes itself known: *Entre le poire et le fromage.* In a meal lacking both pear and cheese, the moment occurs anyway. The translation to American life is that the purpose of the lunch becomes manifest when the main course is consumed but before dessert or coffee are served.

Entre le poire et le fromage

Everyone knows the moment is coming. As the plates are cleared, all parties take a deep breath. The peculiar combination of dread and anticipation causes changes of expression all around the table. There is a prolonged moment of silence and, perhaps, a sigh.

Fingers tense at the edge of the table. Out comes a physical object, drawn from a briefcase or simply taken from an envelope sitting against the leg of someone's chair. The object is often a document of varying size, shape or importance. It may be a catalog or some sheets of paper covered with numbers. At literary lunches, this is the point at which the writer removes the manuscript from his or her pocket or pocketbook.

THE PITCH

The object is placed on the table. It may be placed in the hand of the other luncher or distributed around the table. Nobody seems to want to handle it at first.

An introductory phrase accompanies the document. The most common such phrases are:

"Well…"

"I thought you'd like to have a look at this."

"I've been meaning to ask you..."

"Let me throw something at you."

The object is not actually thrown at the other person. If that should occur, the target has the right to leave the table. The appropriate response to having something thrown at you at lunch is to smile knowingly.

Receiving the Pitch

The receiver of the pitch has two options: Pick it up or leave it alone. A person who picks up the pitch or the object must respond to it. If the meal has been a good one, he probably will, but if the meal has been too good, he will not. This is where Acton's Law of Lunch comes into play: "Absolute Lunch Corrupts Absolutely."

A satiated person does not respond with any intensity to a pitch. It requires too much energy. It might lead to a burp. A satiated person would prefer a cigar or a cognac to a computer print-out.

Responding to a pitch begins with a declaration of innocence. All the hints, plants and forays into the business made earlier in the lunch are forgotten. The object of the pitch feigns surprise:

"My, have you actually written a novel and do you actually have it with you?"

"Really, you've got *pictures* of the DX 7300?"

In spite of the fact that the entire lunch has been

building to this exchange, everyone pretends it hasn't. All persons at the table are instant virgins. This is especially true of seduction lunches, where at least one party will pretend not to know what is going on.

Because the language of business so closely resembles the language of sexual encounter, it is possible to pretend to mistake the meaning of what is being said during a pitch or to double-talk your way knowingly through the rest of the conversation. Any man or woman who wants to discuss "penetration into the market" with a person of the opposite sex at the end of lunch had better clear the calendar for the afternoon.

Sexual or romantic pitches can be direct or indirect.

The direct pitch goes:
"Let's go."

or:

"My place or yours?"
The indirect pitch goes:
"We ought to do this again soon."

or:

"Hey, I have to do some errands on the way back to the office, like check the leak in my ceiling at home. Wanna take a walk with me?"

or:

"What's on your calendar this afternoon?"
The most desperate pitch of this kind ever heard

at lunch was, "Come on. It won't take very long."

Obviously, the best way to deflect an unwelcome sexual pitch is to have a two-thirty appointment.

The Course of Deferred Consideration or the Middle Way: The Tao of Lunch

The essence of the pitch, sexual or commercial, is its rapidity. It comes and goes so quickly that, sometimes, no one notices. The pitch can also be avoided by a wily luncher who pretends to be naive. These people make their concluding remarks as the plates are being cleared, thank their partners for lunch and make their way out of the restaurant with scarcely a glance over their shoulders. "What deal?" they may say later. "Did somebody mention a deal?"

The average response to a pitch is somewhere between picking it up and ignoring it. The pitch remains on the table, to be cleared by the busboy when the tablecloth is removed. That the luncher is taking the Course of Deferred Consideration is made clear by his remark: "I'll get back to you."

"I'll get back to you" is a necessary response because most people at business lunches do not have the power they pretend to have. They could not actually make a decision on the spot even if the chocolate mousse cake moved them to it. Everybody has to check with somebody, and that does not mean in the coatroom. An honest person might admit he lacks the power to decide about the pitch still lying on the table, but, doing so, risks future lunch invitations. Next time, the pitch will go directly to the person he checks with.

People with the power to say anything other than "I'll get back to you" are, at that very moment, lunching in their private dining rooms sixty stories above you. They know they can't go to restaurants because somebody will pitch something at them.

THE MATINEE: SPONTANEOUS DESSERT

The fantasy of having something sexual happen at lunchtime makes lunch worth having. In fact, the ordinary business lunch substitutes the thrill of deal-making for the thrill of sexual spontaneity. Some lines of work require greater sublimation on this score than others. People in the entertainment and communications fields are likely to have sexual escapades in the afternoon because their work schedules are flexible. Financiers, on the other hand, are not. As one Wall Street whiz put it: "The market's only open six hours a day. Why would you want to spend that time in bed with some *girl*?"

Many an afterthought or replay focuses on

The Spontaneous Dessert

sexual possibility not pursued. The luncher relives the moments before dessert, wondering if an opportunity has been missed, imagining what would have happened if only he had said... Most people dismiss the idea as implausible—until the next such lunch—and then pretend that nobody, in fact, actually engages in this sort of activity.

In fact, people do. It is called Spontaneous Dessert and it appears less frequently in times of economic crisis than in times of prosperity, but it does occur. Its relation to the national economy is clarified by understanding that the SD costs both time and money. One thing people mean when they talk about the Good Old Days is the three-to-four-hour lunch in the sack.

Murphy's Matinee

For those who fear they have come on the scene just as the fun has gone out of life, be assured that matinees do still take place. This is how they go:

It takes forever to get the check. The waiter, who has been discreet enough to stay away during the pitch, has lost himself listening to the baseball game on the kitchen radio.

What you thought was a twenty-dollar tip was actually—because of your haste to leave the restaurant—a fifty. You only discover this later.

The captain smiles knowingly, too knowingly, as you leave.

Your boss or his secretary is seated near the door and waves as you go.

There are no empty taxis on the street.

Some people eliminate the taxi problem and save travel time by ducking into a hotel. It takes a self-confident soul to accomplish this, but such people do exist. Ordinary folks are terrified of what they would say to the desk clerk and paralyzed by the idea of needing to check in with luggage so that the enterprise appears respectable. Women are bolder than men at these moments, slapping their credit card down on the hotel desk and commanding a room.

The convenient hotel is always in the best part of town. This puts it in direct proximity to the best restaurants. Some restaurants are actually to be found within hotels. Finding oneself at lunch in a hotel restaurant often makes people wish they had brought along their toothbrushes, just in case, or shaved their legs or canceled their two-thirty appointments.

When the matinee is over, there is a rush for the telephone, both lunchers anxious to reach their secretaries to discover what they have missed and make excuses for their absence.

Returning to the office is mandatory. Everyone

you see, from the elevator starter to your secretary, appears to know where you have been.

THE MOROSE COURSE

By the time coffee comes, it's all over. People sink back at this point much as they did when the meal was served, except they sink deeper. The concept of having won or lost the lunch races through the luncher's mind, often with depressing results. It is possible to have made a sale, made an appointment to meet at the showroom, ironed out a knotty clause in the contract and still feel like a loser. If a celebrity has stopped at the table, greeted your partner with enthusiasm and ignored you, it weighs heavily on your self-esteem. So does feeling boring or fat or pushy or patronized.

During the Morose Course, also known as the "Ain't It Awful?" course, winners and losers alike sigh or grow bleary-eyed. It's all a crock, really. Personal confessions of profound despair fill the air. Someone will say his spouse has left with the cable TV installation man. People admit to sleeping badly and being afraid to walk the streets. There will be a list of friends in the hospital and hitherto-denied symptoms in the speaker himself.

The beach hut will come up. This is the most frequently offered solution to profound despair—the idea of chucking it all and setting up in a fisherman's hut on a Greek island. In Greece, this is the point at which fishermen talk about going to Los Angeles and becoming agents.

The female version of chucking it is moving to the mountains and making quilts. Some women admit to wanting to stay home with babies and soap operas. High-powered female executives express desires to marry zillionaires, spend their days shopping and cease controlling their own lives.

The person who sees himself as the loser of the lunch will most likely initiate the Morose Course, but everyone else gets drawn into it. Often, this coincides with or overlaps the arrival of the check.

Chapter Eight

🍎 ALL LUNCH IS FREE LUNCH 🍎

PRESENTING THE CHECK

The check supposedly appears only when it has been requested. This is not always true in practice. A sales rep who has been waving his hand about emphatically often finds that the waiter has interpreted his gesture as a command for the check. A person gazing morosely into the middle distance often experiences the waiter crossing his line of sight and misunderstanding his glassy stare.

Bringers of checks are notorious for having minds of their own, as

♥ THE LAW OF CHECK PLACEMENT: THE CHECK RESTS ON THE TABLE AT THE FARTHEST POINT FROM THE PERSON WHO IS GOING TO PAY FOR IT.

well as value systems and timetables no one else can decipher. Women are continually unnerved by the refusal of waiters to give them the check when they are lunching with men. In actual practice, checks get set before (1) the tallest person at the table, (2) the fattest person, (3) the oldest or (4) the best dressed. At tables where there is one of each—tall, fat, old and well-dressed—the waiter has a hell of a time.

People either grab the check or ignore it.

Sometimes, the check is presented in a way that makes it impossible to ignore. The arrival of the check in some establishments rivals the presentation of Cherries Jubilee. Checks have been known to come to the table in many different disguises—in secret compartments of leather-bound books or wrapped around the stem of a rose. It has not yet been reported that lunchers receive a check clutched in the hand of a chorus girl leaping from a cake, but that seems perfectly possible. Some restaurants try to make the moment more bearable by including a mint with the check.

The longer the check sits on the table, the more it begins to hum and glow. The people sitting around the check increase their chatter. The check hums louder.

Clubs and private dining rooms spare the luncher. The check never arrives. People with steady lunching places or with foresight never have to see

Presenting the check

the check either. In these situations, the meal simply ends, much as it would at home. There is a certain ease to the checkless finale, but it does eliminate the fun people have when a check is present. And the inexperienced often have trouble figuring out when the lunch is over.

REACHING FOR THE CHECK

*N*o one really pays for lunch. No person, that is, spends actual money for the meal. Business lunching is done on expense accounts, paid for by credit cards or by signing the check, which makes the idea of money extremely remote and the game of pretending to pay extremely hilarious.

The John Hancock

It would seem logical that the top person at a group lunch signs the check, but that rarely happens. One of the marks of a top person is being oblivious to anything that involves money. Bobby Kennedy, for example, had to ask people beside him at church for cash to throw into the collection plate. Bigwigs become babies in the face of a need for cash or a need to pay attention to trivial financial transactions like paying for lunch. It is always the right-hand man who takes on this burden. The signature on the check will belong to the second-in-command.

This does not go smoothly, however, because everyone at the table really *wants* to sign the check. People without check-signing privileges of their own get them by having the check fall beneath their ready pens in a moment of confusion at the end of lunch. Once you have put your signature down, as John Hancock quickly learned, you will be able to do it again and again.

"I'll Take It This Time."

Some people say nothing and simply reach. This can be alarming, particularly if the previous conversation has been along the lines of "Let me throw something at you."

Most people say: "Here, I'll get it" or "Let me" or "I'll take it this time." If the person has lost the lunch and says "I'll get it," he probably refers to what will happen when he tells the boss.

"I'll take it this time" is an invitation to further lunching.

One round of "I'll get it/No, I'll get it" is considered sufficient. Beyond that, the discussion is a barroom brawl, giving the check greater seriousness than it deserves. Since it is simply a matter of whose credit card gets placed on the tray, and since all credit cards look alike, function in the same way, pass through the same accounting procedures and get the same tax write-offs, it hardly seems worth the fuss.

Still, people do reach. Doing so means overcoming obstacles. Knocking over the water glass is common, although some lunchers prefer to knock over the silver vase with the pink rose in it. The hardest situation in which to reach for a check is the tandem table, where you are sitting right beside your lunch partner and the check lies on the other side of him or her. In order to get the check, you must make body contact. This makes lunch appear, momentarily, to be a contact sport.

Sex and Money

The struggle over the check between men and women is more ferocious than it is when two men or two women lunch together. Far more men than one would imagine persist in insisting on paying for a woman. Female executives avoid this contretemps, reminiscent of high school and back seats of cars, by taking men to lunch in places where they have corporate accounts or by arranging to have the check sent to the office.

The Last Resort

Some people, not surprisingly, like to be paid for. If they protest about the check, they do so in the hope that they will be denied. They work hard on developing the right tone of voice in which to insist and be overcome. As a last resort, they turn to the Wyatt Earp Ploy: "If You Don't Want to Pay for Lunch, Pull Out Cash." Cash embarrasses everyone, including the waiters. Some people have not seen cash for years.

TIPPING

*I*n private dining rooms, the subject of tips does not come up. In clubs, the tip is usually automatic. Otherwise, the luncher is required to make a decision.

People who feel they have lost the lunch may, in fact, have won the dubious distinction of paying the check. The tip is their only way of expressing disappointment and anger. In these cases, the tips are small. Large tips usually follow a good lunch or are offered as a bribe by people sitting at bad tables hoping for better ones next time. Lunchers about to become lovers, if they remember to pay the check at all, leave the largest tips.

LEAVING

*L*eaving the restaurant is not like entering it. Lunchers leave together. They observe the room and the room observes them back. Everybody seems to know what has happened. In contrast to the excitement and anxiety of the arrival, the mood of departure ranges from depression and exhaustion to inflated self-esteem and satisfaction bordering on megalomania. One difference between entering and leaving a restaurant is the fact that a meal has been consumed. This means that at least one person will feel larger on leaving lunch than on arriving. Some, however, look curiously deflated.

People seated at the tables lunchers have to pass as they leave the restaurant are experts at interpreting what has happened. That is why they are seated up front. They need only observe the demeanor of the departing lunchers to know whether someone has been hired or fired, received news of a spouse's infidelity or the size of a divorce settlement, or whether the lunchers have argued or fallen in love.

Good observers pay particular attention to what people carry as they leave lunch and how they carry it. If the heavy manila envelope has been passed from one hand to another, a transaction has taken place. People lunching with publishers leave with books in their hands, record people with albums and so on. Since most high-powered exchanges of merchandise take place through messenger services, leaving with the goods brands the lunchers as middle-level employees or thieves. Nobody leaves with a doggie bag, although many feel that they are somehow left holding the bag.

ON THE STREET

*W*hen the lunchers reach the sidewalk, they can part immediately, walk to the corner together, remain together for an hour, an afternoon or the rest of their lives. Lovers, as we have seen, have leaped for taxis or strolled to hotels. When people part after lunch, one may step gingerly into a limousine and offer the other a lift. If he does not offer, the person left on the sidewalk can try to bribe another limo driver or pray that a taxi appears instantly. Just as everyone goes to lunch at the same time, everyone leaves at the same time. Finding an empty taxi is impossible. Two lunchers who need taxis are usually going in opposite directions.

THE OFFICE AGAIN

*I*t has been known to happen that people return to the office together after lunch. When they work in the same office, this is natural. The mood, however, changes as soon as they enter the office building. Someone they have been gossiping about will invariably be in the elevator. If a man and woman have been out to lunch together, their office mates will look them over to see what happened. The expression on the faces of postlunch observers is always: GET ANY?

Bringing a stranger back to the office after lunch is like taking a date home to Mom. This, too, becomes more intense when both sexes are involved. An executive's secretary is bound to be hostile to the lunch companion returning with her boss. If the client has already had a business meeting, been taken to lunch and then reappears, everyone in the office is confused and downright suspicious. In fact, the only time the luncher brings a companion back to the office is when neither party has anything to do for the afternoon. Such carters-about of lunch partners are clinging people who never know when to let go.

THE FAREWELL: ALL LUNCH LEADS TO MORE LUNCH

ost often, a handshake, a peck on the cheek or a thump on the back ends the lunch. There are promises to "do it again soon" and a hasty return, solo, to the office where everything that happened at lunch gets translated into action. The fastest translation is to pick up the telephone and make another lunch date.

Postlunch telephone calls are made to confirm what was found out at lunch, pass it along or talk to someone on the other side of it. For this reason, not only does all lunch lead to more lunch, but, as Sir Isaac Newton so astutely observed: "Every Lunch Has an Equal and Opposite Lunch."

In practice, this means that if you have made a pitch at lunch that led to a sale, the next lunch will be one at which someone pitches you. If you have gossiped about a mutual friend, you will then have lunch with the friend. If someone has complained about your performance, your ability to deliver, the movement on the charts or the penetration into the market, you will then lunch with someone else to whom you can complain about all those things.

If lunch ended in the sack, the next one won't because your partner will be unwilling, the circumstances impossible or because someone saw you do it last time.

If you were sold something at lunch one day, you will sell it to someone else the next or have it stolen from you.

ENDLESS LUNCH

Although it significantly ends the day for people who drink too much, lunch usually reverberates through the afternoon. It reaches all over the world.

🍎 *LUNCH AND TELL*

In the course of the afternoon, lunchers tell someone else:
1. The best joke heard at lunch.
2. A piece of shoptalk or gossip, but only enough to imply they know more than they are willing to let on.
3. The name of the lunch partner or the name of any person present in the restaurant or the name of anyone mentioned in the course of the conversation.
4. The name of the restaurant eaten in or the names of all the restaurants considered.

Lunch pursues you all day long. British friends ask advice about something that came up during their lunch while you are still taking your morning coffee. Los Angeles associates share their lunch news as you are thinking about cocktails. People call up from the Sun Belt bursting to tell you what they heard at lunch. You listen with envy to the golf sounds in the background, the suntans on the wire, and pull off your galoshes.

THE MOMENT OF TRUTH: THE T&E

*J*ust when you think you have forgotten lunch, the moment of truth appears. This is known as the T&E. It is the moment you fill out your expense account, try to find all those receipts and search your memory for just what urgent business it was that drove you to "21" three times in a week. You may remember but be unable to say.

Nearly everyone who goes in for big-time lunching has an emergency list of names that come to life only on expense forms. These names are usually filed at the back of the Rolodex under *X*. Who these people are varies from one industry to another. For publishers, it is a list of California literary agents. Elsewhere, the list contains names of branch managers and taxi dispatchers. Low-scale celebrity names will do in a pinch. Free-lance hustlers are always useful.

It is smart to keep the list current and pay particular attention to the obituary columns on this score. You will find that there are, everywhere in the world, people willing to let their good names be used for just such purposes. Such people demand payment. Payment is always—of course—a lunch.

*S*ince everybody does it, there must be something to it.

Fashions change, markets plunge, hemlines rise, waistbands tighten, but lunch goes on. Those who didn't suddenly do, those who did abruptly desist, bad ones get better at it, good ones give lessons in it, but there is always lunch.

Corporate vice-presidents and restaurant headwaiters may change places, the population may drift to the Sun Belt, Italians may outlaw it and Arabs import it, but nobody eliminates lunch. If women do it more confidently, homosexuals more openly and minorities more regularly, lunch still goes on. Therefore it is a good idea to know something about it.

Perhaps the most important of the conclusions drawn in this book is the remark made by a wise man named Heisenberg. Drawing philosophically upon his cigar as lunch came to its end, he said: "Any Observation of Lunch Changes the Lunch Itself."

This passed into history as Heisenberg's Uncertainty Principle. His companion, interestingly enough, was the poet Tennyson who, it is said, replied: "It Is Better to Have Lunched and Lost Than Never to Have Lunched at All."